A 1958 Vespa GS (VS4). It has a locking glove box, spare wheel and auxiliary fuel tank mounted inside the spare wheel.

MOTOR SCOOTERS

Expanded second edition

Michael Webster

A Shire book

CONTENTS

*Published in 2007 by Shire Publications Ltd,
Cromwell House, Church Street, Princes
Risborough, Buckinghamshire HP27 9AA, UK.
Copyright © 1986 and 2007 by Michael Webster.
First published 1986; reprinted 1992. Second,
enlarged edition, 2007. Shire Album 181. ISBN
978 0 7478 0668 4.*

Printed in Great Britain by Ashford Colour Press Ltd, Unit 600, Fareham Reach, Fareham Road, Gosport, Hampshire PO13 0FW.

Editorial Consultant: Michael E. Ware, former Curator of the National Motor Museum, Beaulieu.

British Library Cataloguing in Publication Data: Webster, Michael. Motor scooters. – 2nd ed. – (Shire album; 181) 1. Motor scooters – History I. Title 629.2'275 ISBN-13: 978 0 7478 0668 4.

ACKNOWLEDGEMENTS

I would like to thank all those who have helped to make this Album possible and especially Glynn Millhouse for his photographic assistance, Jill Crerar for her patience in typing and correcting the manuscript, and Bill Drake for general assistance and encouragement. The help of Ian Harrop, Dominique Warin, Alex Brett, Goran Hellsin, Kev Walsh, Bob Coult, Howard Chambers, Robin Spalding, Kees Portange, David Endean (Bikers Ltd), Paul Styles (Doble Motorcycles) and Mike Hayman is gratefully acknowledged as is the help of the National Motor Museum, the Science Museum and the Imperial War Museum.

Illustrations on the following pages are acknowledged to: the Imperial War Museum, pages 8, 9 (lower left and right); the Science Museum, page 5 (lower). All other illustrations, including the cover picture, are from the author's collection.

COVER: *A 1952 125cc Douglas Vespa and a 1959 200cc Durkopp Diana.*

LEFT: *The British-made Triumph Tigress scooter was sold in the late 1950s and early 1960s as a 175 cc two-stroke or 250 cc four-stroke twin.*

This 1956 Imperial sidecar connected to a Lambretta Model LD is typical of the mid 1950s style of machine.

INTRODUCTION

To many people the word 'scooter' conjures up pictures of the small-wheeled, brightly coloured machines that appeared in large numbers throughout the 1950s. Although the 1950s and 1960s were the period of the largest scooter sales, this was the second generation of scooters. The first scooters appeared between 1916 and 1924, when a number of small, sometimes crude machines enjoyed considerable, if brief success.

Whilst the motorcycle has shown a steady development of the original theme without radical change, the development of the scooter involved designers with no motorcycle background and no preconceived ideas as to what form their creations should take. The result was that, in a few years, machines appeared with almost every conceivable shape and transmission system. Many ingenious suspension systems evolved and for the first time motors were specifically designed to fit the machines, a reversal of general motorcycle practice.

3

This Hildebrand and Wolfmueller of 1894 shows several design features common to most scooters. Note the open-frame design and small rear wheel.

THE EARLY YEARS

There has been considerable speculation as to when the scooter first appeared, rather like the various claims for the first motor car. Though claims for several manufacturers may be considered, one of the earliest machines with scooter features was the Hildebrand and Wolfmueller dating from 1894. This machine was built in Munich and France up to 1896 and sold in reasonable quantities. The Hildebrand was equipped with a two-cylinder four-stroke motor, of 90 mm bore and 117 mm stroke. Wheel sizes were 26 inches (660 mm) at the front and 22 inches (559 mm) at the rear, with solid tyres, and the rear mudguard was constructed to form a semicircular tank filled with water that was piped to the cylinders for cooling. The motor had an automatic inlet valve and a mechanical exhaust valve controlled by a cam on the rear wheel hub. The surface-type carburettor had a handlebar-controlled mixture valve

and the hot-tube ignition was operated via a spirit burner located just behind the headstock. The machine held lubricating oil in the frame tubes and had a speed range of between 3 and 24 mph (5 to 38 km/h).

The first generation of scooters in any quantity appeared some years later. From 1916 until approximately 1924 keen interest in scooters led to the introduction of the Autoped, the Grigg, the Autoglider, the Kingsbury, the Skootamota, the Unibus, the Stafford Pup and many more.

Most of the early scooters were of dubious design and practicality. The Autoped, for example, which originated in the United States, was made under licence in England and Germany (in Germany it was known as the Krupp). This machine had a 155 cc motor mounted on the nearside of the front wheel with a direct drive. The clutch and

ABOVE LEFT: *The Autoped from 1916 was driven in a standing position. The steering column served as clutch and brake. Pushed forward, the drive was engaged. Pulled back, the drive disengaged and the brake was applied.*

ABOVE RIGHT: *The Autoglider was advertised as the 'Little Aristocrat' with the sales slogan 'the machine which gives the maximum amount of comfort and reliability for the minimum expenditure'. The 2.75 horsepower machine was priced at 55 guineas in 1920.*

BELOW: *The ABC Skootamota originated in 1919 and, when first tested, had a speed varying from 2 to 15 mph (3 to 24 km/h).*

The Unibus of 1920 shows remarkably modern styling but was offered at £99 15s, a price that few could afford.

front brake were both operated by moving the steering column forward or backwards; as the machine was ridden from a standing position this gave the rider a very insecure feeling. Many of the early scooters were no more than motorised versions of the toy scooter and, as in the Autoped, had an engine mounted and driving directly on the front wheel.

C. E. Johns of Alvis fame produced one such model, known as the Stafford Pup. Whilst the machine itself had little to recommend it, the motor was of an advanced design with overhead valves and a capacity of 142 cc. Almost all the weight on this machine was on the left-hand side of the front wheel and the frame possessed little rigidity, particularly in the headstock area. It is, perhaps, fortunate that only a small number were built and sold.

Kingsbury Aviation of Croydon made a better designed machine, the attractive and ingenious little Kingsbury scooter, which had a two-stroke, mid-mounted motor in a well constructed ladder-style frame, driving the rear wheel by a conventional chain complete with tensioner. Two-wheel braking was provided and the front suspension consisting of spring sliders proved simple and effective. Both the Kingsbury and the Stafford Pup offered a

The Stafford Pup from 1920 offered an advanced four-stroke overhead-valve motor of 1.75 horsepower but the flimsy frame structure and standing riding position were less than ideal. This machine has solid tyres but most Pups were sold with inflatable tyres.

The Reynolds Runabout had a 269 cc Wall Liberty engine with separate petrol and oil tanks carried behind the front shield. The gearbox was a two-speed Moss with a choice of either all-chain or belt drive. The tyre size was 24 by 2½ inches (610 by 64 mm).

pillar-mounted seat as an alternative to the standing position.

Of the numerous designs that quickly came and went, two machines are of special interest. The ABC Skootamota had a practical mechanical arrangement and provided an economical form of transport. A compact horizontal 155 cc motor with overhead inlet and side exhaust valves was mounted above the rear wheel, driving it via a clutch and reduction gear. Skootamota's machines sold in considerable numbers and many still exist.

The Unibus, built in 1920 by the Gloucester Aircraft Company, was perhaps the most interesting design of all the early scooters. It was designed by Harold D. Boultebee and would appear to be the earliest example of a totally enclosed scooter, providing for the first time full weather protection, with a styling more appropriate to the 1950s than to 1920. Technically the Unibus was equally advanced, with a 269 cc two-stroke engine mounted vertically behind the front wheel and driving through a shaft to a worm-wheel housing at the rear. A car-type starting handle projected from the rear of the leg shield, whilst the two-speed gearbox gave a top speed of approximately 26 mph (42 km/h). At £99 15s the Unibus was too expensive and, whilst it deserved to succeed, it was too far ahead of its time to be appreciated fully. The general public had also become extremely wary about scooters as more than a dozen models had been rushed on to the market since 1918 and many of these were crude, uncomfortable and difficult to handle.

By the mid 1920s interest in the motor scooter had died and sales were non-existent. With the exception of one or two of the early machines, motor scooters had proved woefully inadequate and many people saw them as a joke.

A Welbike being removed from the special container used for dropping by parachute. Note the absence of gears, mudguards and front brake.

SCOOTERS AT WORK AND AT WAR

Many of the scooters built between 1915 and 1924 were ridden by ladies. However, the Second World War created a need for a small mechanical means of transport for troops in situations where it was impracticable to provide jeeps or full-size motorcycles.

The scooter returned in 1942 in the form of the Welbike manufactured by the Excelsior Motor Company in Birmingham. It was designed by Harry Lester at a military design and research establishment under the direction of Lieutenant Colonel J. R. V. Dolphin. It was called 'Welbike' because the prototype was constructed at Welwyn in Hertfordshire. The machine was constructed so that it would fold and fit into a specially designed canister to be dropped by parachute alongside the troops.

Although extremely small, the Welbike was capable of carrying considerable loads with its 98 cc Villiers power unit and very simple construction. The machine had no gearbox and no front brake but had a range of over 90 miles (145 km). In order to keep the profile low the petrol tanks were pannier-mounted and, in the absence of gravity feed, required a small hand pump to pressurise them. This little machine could achieve 30 mph (48 km/h) and weighed less than 70 pounds (31.7 kg). Four thousand Welbikes were supplied to the War Department and were used in action in Europe and the Far East. Welbikes were also carried ashore by the troops during the D-Day landings in Normandy in 1944 and some went to Russia.

Wartime scooters were also produced in Italy, Germany and the United States. From 1944 the American Cushman Motor Works of Nebraska manufactured several versions of a scooter which could be dropped by parachute. The Cushman 53 was larger and heavier than the Welbike, with a four-stroke 244 cc engine, two-speed transmission and speed

ABOVE: *Two variations of the Welbike. The folded model is a standard Mark I whilst the other is one of the prototypes.*

BELOW LEFT: *United States Army and Navy guards with a Cushman scooter in North Africa, August 1943.*

BELOW RIGHT: *Allied soldiers using a captured Volugrafo Aermoto for a day out in Rome in 1944. The twin front wheels were normal on this model.*

9

capability of approximately 40 mph (64 km/h). Unlike the Welbike, the Cushman did not fold or have a container but it was constructed to withstand the impact of landing and carried direct attachment points for the parachute. More than four thousand machines were produced between 1944 and 1945. These were used in Holland, France and other western European countries.

Italy produced a machine that was intermediate between the Welbike and the Cushman, having folding handlebars as in the Welbike, but with parachute attachment points like the Cushman. The machine was produced by Societa Volugrafo in Turin and was named the Aermoto. This scooter consisted of a 125 cc single-port two-stroke engine with a two-speed gearbox providing speeds up to 40 mph (64 km/h). Several of these machines were captured by the Allied forces in their advance through Italy in 1944-5.

By the end of the Second World War the scooter had proved to be an economical and viable method of transport. In the austerity of the post-war period, therefore, many people turned to the scooter as a cheap and reliable means of

This early Brockhouse Corgi has wire wheels but in production these were quickly changed to disc-type wheels. This machine is a single-speed model with no kick-start; the Mark IV Corgi had a kick-start and two-speed gear.

10

A Mark II Swallow Gadabout from 1951. This model had foot gear change, front suspension and pivoting rear bodywork for accessibility. The motor was a 125 cc Villiers unit and a commercial box sidecar version was available. The manufacturers were the famous Swallow Coachworks responsible for Jaguar cars.

travel. This need was satisfied in Britain initially by a civilian copy of the military Welbike known as the Corgi, manufactured by Brockhouse Engineering near Southport, Merseyside. The first Corgi appeared in 1946, the major change from the Welbike being that the fuel tank was larger and mounted centrally above the motor. The similarity with the Welbike was apparent in that it had a rigid construction and a 98 cc horizontal engine, in this case an Excelsior Spryt, but still no gearbox.

Other machines were to follow, such as the Swallow, BAC Gazelle and Bond Minibike. The Swallow Gadabout was even produced with a commercial box attached, which proved very popular for local deliveries. Scooters at this time had little or no recreational purpose but were seen simply as an efficient and inexpensive means of transport for business purposes. This was soon to change when brightly coloured and stylish scooters emerged from engineering works in Italy and other countries where work forces could no longer be employed on military production.

The Triumph T10 of 1965 was a slightly revised Triumph Tina. Minor mechanical changes were introduced, together with bright metallic red paintwork and extra chromium, to improve flagging sales.

A standard 123 cc Lambretta of 1951. Before this period Lambrettas were open-framed and did not use fan cooling. A luxury enclosed version of this machine (LC) was to set the trend for future models.

A SECOND GENERATION:
VESPA AND LAMBRETTA

Although scooters had been out of production from the mid 1920s until the Second World War, their comic image persisted so that when they reappeared they were again disparaged. In retrospect it can be seen that this short-sighted attitude was very costly, particularly for established motorcycle manufacturers, who were slow to adapt to the change in consumer demand. By the time the majority of them had recognised that scooters offered enormous sales opportunities, it was too late to react effectively.

After 1945, two names were to become synonymous with scooters, Vespa and Lambretta. The common characteristics of these two machines were that they were simple, inexpensive, reliable and colourful. The engineering principles behind them were, however, quite different.

VESPA

Piaggio (an aeroplane manufacturer) produced the Vespa and, with the exception of the first hundred machines made in 1945, created a design so advanced in construction and style that the basic layout remains unchanged today. Comparison of a Vespa from the mid 1980s with one from the late 1940s shows that the monocoque structure and engine gearbox layout are very similar, whilst the styling has evolved rather than been re-designed (a reflection on the quality of the original design). By the early 1950s Vespas were being sold in most countries throughout the world. Some were direct Piaggio imports but many were being manufactured under licence in local factories.

In the United Kingdom, Douglas in Bristol manufactured their own version of the 125 cc Italian machine, the most significant change being that the headlamp had to be moved from its Italian position, on the front mudguard, to the front apron in order to be at the height stipulated by British lighting regulations. This machine had a left-hand handlebar gear change controlling the three-speed through a series of rods, ball joints and

bell cranks and became affectionately known by its owners as the 'rod model'. The rod model sold very well in its metallic light green between 1951 and 1953 before being superseded by the model G with a simpler gear-change mechanism consisting of two cables in place of the complicated rod structure. Both the rod model and the G had a single-transfer port motor of 124.8 cc giving 4.5 brake horsepower and 42 mph (67 km/h), but in 1954 the model GL2 was announced, with an entirely new twin-transfer port motor of 123.67 cc, giving 5 brake horsepower. The GL2 looked similar to its predecessors but in February 1955 it was replaced by the 42L2.

The 42L2 headlamp had moved to the handlebars and the overall styling was much tidier, with various colours now being offered. The motor was essentially the GL2 unit and only minor improvements (a larger petrol tank and extended rubber trim on the footboards) were necessary from 1956 to February 1959, when the 152L2 was introduced. The 152L2 had few parts in common with the earlier models and offered better performance, concealed cables and easier kick-start.

In 1955 one of the most exciting Vespas was introduced, the GS or Grand Sport (VS1), made in and imported from Italy, unlike the British-built 125 cc machines. The GS had a 145 cc motor in a different chassis, producing a performance that was considered sensational in 1955. The GS evolved through the VS2, VS3 and VS4 until 1959, when the last of the 150 GS Vespas, known as the VS5, was introduced. This model, whilst identical bodily to its predecessors, had many detail alterations, including different wheel and hub arrangements and new saddle and speedometer design. The VS5 was to continue in production until 1963. The 150 Grand Sport was always sold in one colour only, metallic silver grey, and is still widely regarded as the classic Vespa.

In 1963 the 160 GS, with altered chassis, styling and motor, was produced. The handlebars, wheels and hubs were borrowed from the VS5, but the mechanical parts were new and formed the basis of all subsequent Vespas. In 1966 the top model became the 180 SS, which had a different chassis again, slightly more angular styling and an engine that was effectively an enlarged 160. The headlamp was unusual in that it was trapezium-shaped. The 180 SS finally evolved into the 200 cc Rally, which had electronic ignition, making it a very powerful, reliable long-distance machine.

13

The 125 cc Douglas Vespa was a British-built version of the Italian model. These were the first Vespas to be sold in Britain and with Lambretta LDs set the fashion for all future machines. This 1951 model has a linkage of rods and bell cranks between the handlebars and the rear-mounted gearbox. This was soon changed to the simpler and cheaper cable linkage that is still used. Top speed was 42 mph (67 km/h).

The 90SS was a high-performance, four-gear version of the Vespa 90. The leg shields and handlebars were much narrower than on the standard machine and it also had a dummy tank (glove box), spare wheel and extra storage inside the spare wheel. The high-performance motor and small dimensions made it a much sought-after machine.

There have been numerous variations since the introduction of the Rally and Vespas have continued in production in various forms since 1945.

The Vespa 90SS created great controversy in competition. Club riders were always demanding higher performance models and when Vespa introduced the 90SS this became the machine for competitive riding in road trials, gymkhanas and racing. In the early 1960s Vespa had developed a very narrow, lightweight machine with either a 50 cc or a 90 cc three-speed engine. They made the 90SS narrower still, with a dummy petrol tank (in effect a glove box) located between the nose of the seat and the handlebars.

When introduced in 1967, with its special high-performance engine and four-speed gearbox, the 90SS offered a performance equivalent to some 200 cc scooters, with a manoeuvrability superior to all the bigger machines. The machine was excellent for competition use but there were attempts to have it banned from scooter events on the basis that a scooter, by definition, must have an open frame between the seat and the handlebars. The controversy was ended when the Federation of British Scooter Clubs ruled that the 90SS was a scooter because the glove box, whilst closing the gap, was non-structural and therefore did not constitute an infringement of scooter regulations.

A Lambretta A model from 1947 with 7 inch (178 mm) wheels and no rear suspension. The compartment beneath the pillion seat is a glove box and the gear change is by rocking pedal with a gear indicator on the inside of the right foot board.

LAMBRETTA

Innocenti, in developing the Lambretta, have followed a more varied development programme and their models were designated by letters in the early days, starting with the first Lambretta, the model A.

The Lambretta A, of 1947, was an open-frame scooter with an unenclosed engine and 7 inch (178 mm) wheels. The leg shields were modest, offering much less weather protection than the Vespa, and, unlike the Vespa, there was no rear suspension. The frame was a combination of box-section pressed steel and tubes, whilst the gear change for the 123 cc shaft-drive motor was foot-operated, with an indicator to inform the rider which gear was selected.

In 1948 the B model arrived, looking very similar to the A, but with rear suspension worked by a swinging knuckle on the rear of the shaft drive, controlled by a coil-spring damper located horizontally under the motor. The gear-change mechanism on the B was moved to the left hand on a twist-grip arrangement using a single teleflex (push/pull) cable.

In 1951 a new all-tubular frame design using a single large-diameter main tube and trailing-link front suspension, both of which have been characteristics of almost

The Lambretta B (1948), whilst visually similar to the A, has 8 inch (203 mm) wheels, rear suspension and hand gear change via a teleflex cable.

TOP: *The Lambretta Li150 Series II is one of the best known machines. They sold in vast quantities in the early 1960s and epitomised the qualities of the scooter.*

CENTRE: *The 75 cc Lambretta Cometa introduced separate oil lubrication and caused a sensation with its striking 'Bertone' styling in 1969. Performance was outstanding with a top speed of above 55 mph (88 km/h).*

BOTTOM: *The 125 cc Piatti was an Italian design built under licence in Britain and Belgium. This machine, manufactured by Cyclemaster (Britax), had a wide range of accessories including a front-mounted shopping rack and spare wheel with stowage above. The stand was lowered by pulling a knob on the dash panel and tyre size was 3½ by 7 inches (89 by 178 mm).*

TOP: *The Puch Alpine 150 had a capacity of 147 cc, producing 6 horsepower. The wheel size was 3¼ by 12 inches (83 by 305 mm) and the machine was capable of 53 mph (85 km/h). This 1959 Austrian scooter was available with an electric starter or kick-start.*

CENTRE: *The Progress of 1956 had its origins in the Strolch from Germany. The motor was a 191 cc Sachs unit with electric start and automatic neutral selection. Tyre size was 3¼ by 16 inches (83 by 406 mm) and the price when new was £229 8s.*

BOTTOM: *This Bastert was a luxury scooter dating from 1951. The motor was a JLO 175 cc with a top speed of 50 mph (80 km/h).*

The Lambretta LD150 was an extremely popular machine from 1954 to 1959. This model has shaft drive and torsion-bar rear suspension and was available with many extras including a clock, a petrol gauge and even a radio.

all subsequent Lambretta models, was introduced. The model C provided a new chassis for essentially the same engine as the model B (5 horsepower) and was still an open-frame design with minimal leg shielding.

The popularity of Lambretta in Britain grew with the introduction of the LC, which was a totally enclosed version of the C. This total enclosure was achieved by having a new rear body section with side panels and leg shields of full height and wider than those fitted to the C. The body design of the LC was carried through to its successor, the LD, in 1954, but the mechanical aspects were diffe-rent.

Under the LC-style skin the LD had a totally different engine and frame, which allowed the motor to pivot in one solid mass to form the rear suspension via a torsion-bar link. Capacity increased to 148 cc, although 123 cc versions were still available, and the front suspension springs were enclosed in the front fork tubes and not externally as in the C. The L designation on the LC and LD stood for luxury, indicating that they offered more than the basic models, and a D model was offered alongside the LD retaining the new mechanical features in an open-style frame. The LD had enor-

Sir Bernard and Lady Docker with the ill-fated BSA Beeza scooter, 1955. Only a handful of this 200 cc side-valve electric-start machine were produced; performance was very poor and volume production never started.

TOP: *A Dunkley Popular with a four-stroke 49 cc overhead-valve motor producing 2 brake horsepower. This 1959 machine had a top speed of 34 mph (55 km/h) and cost £76 2s 7d when new.*

CENTRE: *In 1960 Ambassador Motor Cycles produced this Villiers 173 cc scooter. For many years Ambassador was the Zundap distributor in Britain and this scooter clearly resembles the Zundap Bella. The 12 inch (305 mm) wheels are cast aluminium and the dashboard carries a low fuel level light.*

BOTTOM: *This 1951 Mors Speed from France has a cast aluminium main frame with a two-speed 115 cc two-stroke motor. Gears are selected by two heel pedals.*

mous sales up to 1959 when the Mark IV derivative of the LD was sold alongside the first of the TV and Li series, one version being available with an electric start.

The production of machines fell out of sequence when the E and F model Lambrettas were produced in the 1951-4 period, but they had poor sales (the E having a hand-recoil starter).

The first four-speed Lambretta (previously all had been three-gear), the luxury TV175, was introduced in 1957. This machine was totally new in design, and wheel size increased from 4 by 8 inches (102 by 203 mm) to 3½ by 10 inches (89 by 254 mm). Shaft drive gave way to totally enclosed duplex chain and the engine was horizontal, swung in conjunction with a coil-spring damper arrangement to form the rear suspension. The front mudguard was fixed, unlike all its predecessors, which had turned with the front wheel. The TV175 (designation TV1) had a capacity of 170 cc and provided 8.6 horsepower. Although well received, it was expensive and had several niggling weaknesses with a record for unreliability. The design, however, was not wasted because in 1958 the Li Series 1 appeared.

The Li Series 1 owed its body style to the TV1 but it had a new engine design. The Li was produced as a 125 cc (6.5 horsepower) or 150 cc (7.5 horsepower) model and sold in vast quantities. Lambretta had eliminated all the problems inherent in the TV1 and the reliability of

the Li has never been suspect. With four gears, larger wheels and much better performance, the Li Series proved to be comfortable and ideal for general use.

In 1959 Lambretta introduced the Li Series 2, the most significant modification being the moving of the headlamp from the front apron to the handlebars so that it turned with the steering. The demand for more power resulted in a TV 175 (175 cc) version (designation TV2) which was not a recreation of the TV1 but an enlarged capacity Li2. Changes were made to gear ratios dependent on engine capacity and these became quite complex in later years when Lambretta introduced various capacity models to suit different applications. In 1962 rebodied Li and TV Series machines were introduced as 'slim-style' models. The new bodies were narrower and more angular and the shape was to last without substantial modification into the mid 1980s.

The 175 slimstyle (TV3), was extremely popular with scooter clubs as it had a high performance (8.7 horsepower), excellent handling, disc front brake and front dampers (not fitted to Li Series 3) but in Britain there were constant demands for yet more power. Though based in Milan, Innocenti regarded the United Kingdom as a very important scooter market and produced a special model for Britain known as the GT. This model was not initially available in Italy, where the largest capacity was still 175 cc, but it was effectively a TV3 with a 200 cc engine and restyled side panels and colour scheme.

The top speed was over 70 mph (113 km/h) and from then on Lambretta were always to offer 200 cc models for the British market. Variations on the slim-style base produced the Pacemaker and GP models, some having electronic ignition and most being available in three engine capacities, 125 cc, 150 cc and 200 cc. In Britain the 175 cc capacity was discontinued soon after the introduction of the GT in 1964.

Lambretta produced two other scooter families of note, the first being the J series. The J range was based on a monocoque steel chassis unit with a vertical single-cylinder motor in 50 cc, 100 cc and 125 cc versions.

The second and more unusual range of scooters was the Luna series styled by Bertone. There were three models, the 50 cc Lui, the 75 cc Vega and the 75 cc Cometa (the last having separate oil feed via a tank and oil pump). Performance of the 75 cc Vega was impressive, with a top speed of 55 mph (89 km/h) from 5.2

horsepower. The lightweight, space-age styling and high ground clearance made it a very popular machine, rivalling the 90SS Vespa in trials and gymkhanas. Innocenti was taken over by British Leyland and subsequently, with the decline in scooter sales, all production ceased in the early 1970s. Like Vespa, however, Innocenti had sold manufacturing rights to various countries and Indian or Spanish Lambrettas continued in production. Unfortunately, the range was rationalised to one basic model with various engine capacities (GP 125, 150 or 200) and they survived for only a few more years.

Since 1950, while Lambretta and Vespa had the vast majority of scooter sales, more than two hundred other manufacturers attempted to capture a market share. Many famous names like Harley Davidson, Motoguzzi, BSA and BMW brought out models but only a handful of makes achieved even reasonable sales and some were a financial disaster.

DESIGN AND INGENUITY

The appearance of the motor scooter was of great importance both to the purchaser and to the manufacturer, and the all-enveloping bodywork gave designers great scope for individuality.

The more traditional engineering companies made tubular frames, as in motorcycle practice, and in many cases used motorcycle engines also. Around these fairly conventional structures, flowing body curves of bewildering variety appeared. Some companies used glass-fibre bodywork and many others used cast aluminium, sheet aluminium, steel and even magnesium. Some manufacturers showed a more innovative approach and several monocoque designs were produced, the most famous being the Vespa. Another Italian manufacturer, Moto Rumi (which during the Second World War had made midget submarines), used a structure wholly of cast aluminium in which the motor crankcase formed the centre section of the frame.

Scooters were always at the forefront of technological innovation. For example,

disc brakes were introduced to Lambrettas in the very early 1960s, long before the motorcycle industry considered their widespread use. Water cooling, widely accepted in motorcycles only in the 1980s, was introduced in the French PP Roussey scooter in 1954, whilst shaft drive (Lambretta) or direct-gear drive (Vespa) removed the necessity for the adjustment of dirty chains as early as 1947. In later years Lambretta did use a chain, but it was totally enclosed and did not require adjustment, lubrication or cleaning.

Several companies manufactured scooters with either preselector gearboxes or automatic transmission. The French used preselection on the Scooterrot, whilst a variable-belt automatic transmission system was incorporated in such scooters as the DKW (Manhurin) Hobby and the Triumph Tina. Other manufacturers retained conventional gearboxes but even these often incorporated automatic neutral selectors, warning lights to indicate when neutral was engaged, or, in the case

TOP: *This Moto Rumi was sold in three versions, all with a 124.68 cc twin-cylinder two-stroke motor. Power output varied from 6.5 to 8.5 horsepower with the top speed on the twin-carburettor Bol d'Or version being around 75 mph (120 km/h). In 1960 this all cast alloy machine cost £209 5s 8d.*

UPPER CENTRE: *The Lambretta TV175 (Series 3) of 1962 was the first model to incorporate a disc front brake. The basic styling of all subsequent Lambrettas followed this example.*

LOWER CENTRE: *The Manhurin Concorde was a German DKW Hobby built under licence in France in the 1960s. It had a two-stroke 74 cc motor producing 3 brake horsepower with a hand-pull starter and fully automatic variable pulley-belt transmission.*

BOTTOM: *The Maico Mobil was originally produced as a 175 cc machine but most were 200 cc. In the 1950s this machine was advertised as a 'car on two wheels'. The aluminium bodywork was fitted over a space-frame chassis providing excellent comfort and weather protection.*

TOP: *The FMC was identical to the French Peugeot scooter and made under licence. Note the opening storage compartment on the nose of the machine and the clips to anchor further luggage on the nose. This model was available in 1957 as a 125 cc or a 147 cc machine and on both versions suspension was by rubber band. Maximum speed for the 125 cc was 51 mph (82 km/h).*

UPPER CENTRE: *The Velocette Viceroy of 1962 has a 250 cc horizontally opposed two-stroke twin motor with reed-valve induction. The motor is mounted behind the front wheel with a shaft drive to the four-speed gearbox mounted in the rear hub. Tyre size is 4 by 12 inches (102 by 305 mm).*

LOWER CENTRE: *The Terrot of 1953 was a product of the famous French motorcycle manufacturer. This machine is a two-speed 125 cc model which was also sold as the Magnat-debon. Scooterrot versions were later imported to Britain by Phelon and Moore (Panther) and featured a three-speed pre-selector gearbox.*

BOTTOM: *A TWN Contessa of 1956. This luxury German scooter had a 197 cc all-aluminium split single two-stroke engine and four gears. A top speed of 65 mph (105 km/h) was achievable and standard equipment included spare wheel, neutral selector and electric starter.*

The 1954 PP Roussey from France had a horizontal 170 cc water-cooled two-stroke motor and three gears. The radiator is mounted in the front leg shield.

of Maicos, a speedometer-mounted gear indicator.

With most scooters, spare wheels were available and capable of being carried on the machine. Some manufacturers designed the scooters to house the spare wheel as an integral part of the body, with car-type wheel mountings that made wheel replacement very simple, even on a dark night.

Many machines were designed with integral luggage-carrying capacity, like the Maico Mobil, which had two large panniers as part of the rear bodywork, reached by lifting an aluminium pressing that also served to support the pillion seat. Luggage space was to be found in every conceivable location. The Peugeot Elite possessed a front-mounted boot, the Heinkel came equipped with a front-mounted carrier and NSU provided storage space behind the leg shields.

Many scooters were created as a total concept, whereby the engine and transmission system were designed specifically to fit the machine. The result of this approach was that engines were mounted in many different locations and were in some cases of radical design. Velocette, in designing the Viceroy, wanted good

A 1952 Ducati Cruiser of very advanced design. The scooter had a 175 cc overhead-valve electric start motor producing 7.5 horsepower and was made by the famous Ducati Motor Cycle Company in Italy.

24

A 1956 Faka Commodore with a JLO 197 cc motor developing 9.3 brake horsepower. Hydraulic coupled brakes were a feature of this 58 mph (93 km/h) scooter.

balance with a low centre of gravity. They produced a horizontally opposed reed-valve, two-stroke twin engine and mounted this transversely, immediately behind the front wheel of the machine. From the rear of this motor a shaft took the power to a gearbox mounted in the rear hub. Many manufacturers designed the engine and rear suspension of the machine as a single unit, as in all Vespas and most Lambrettas. The German Triumph Company (known in Great Britain as TWN to avoid confusion with the English Triumph Motor Cycle Company) used this method in their Contessa whilst French manufacturers favoured rubber-band suspension.

A basic design feature of scooters was built-in weather protection and one model, the Maico Mobil, was advertised as a car on two wheels. This machine and several others were designed to include a windscreen, not as an extra, but as an integral part of the machine.

Scooters were available in a choice of bright colours, and manufacturers and independent accessory companies marketed a host of extras so that machines could be personalised to suit the buyer's individual needs.

The 1951 Pirol was an eye-catching scooter. The motor was a 200 cc 6.5 horsepower two-stroke with a top speed of 50 mph (80 km/h). Note the interesting trailing-arm front suspension.

A PP Roussey racing at Montlhery.

TRIALS AND ACHIEVEMENTS

In 1955 the first sports scooters made their appearance and this development very quickly led to scooter racing. In June 1955 scooters first appeared at Montlhery in the Criterion de France event with both sports and standard machines. In both the 125 cc sport and standard classes the winners were French scooters made by Mors. In the sports class the winner was Nebout, with an average speed of 77.106 km/h (48 mph), whilst Lavialle won the standard class with a speed of 73.975 km/h (46 mph). Both these machines were very close to being standard scooters and were followed by many LD Lambrettas.

In the prestigious Bol d'Or of 1955, two Frenchmen, Daric and Brugeilles, finished first in their class with a 150 cc Lambretta, covering 1508 km (937 miles) at an average of 62.868 km/h (39.025 mph). The Bol d'Or, whilst officially a speed trial, was undoubtedly the two-wheel equivalent of the Le Mans 24-hour car race. The only important modifications made to the machines of Daric and Brugeilles were a special cylinder head, a racing carburettor with a 23 mm choke and an extra fuel tank.

By 1956 the Daric/Brugeilles Lambretta had increased the 24-hour distance to 1948 km (1210.5 miles) and the average speed had risen to 81.179 km/h (50.44 mph). The scooters raced were still almost standard models and out of five scooters starting the race four completed it. In the sports class, a Moto Rumi ridden by Cambis and Ditail won, with an average speed of 71.355 km/h (44.34 mph), in spite of some trouble. This performance by Rumi scooters was the first of a succession of victories by them in the Bol d'Or event.

In 1957 Rumi took the first two places

26

A 125 cc Mors Paris Nice that formed the basis for numerous 1955 racing scooters in France. Front suspension is by rubber band.

in the racing class but it was not until 1958 that 125 cc scooters were allowed to race in a 125 cc class (previously they were competing against 175 cc machines). In the 175 cc racing class, a water-cooled PP Roussey ridden by the Terrioux brothers won, with an average speed of 81.775 km/h (50.81 mph), whilst in the 125 cc racing class the best performance ever by a scooter was achieved by Foidelli and Bois with a distance of 2095 km (1302.2 miles) and an average speed of 87.327 km/h (54.258 mph).

The first British scooter race took place at Crystal Palace on 4th July 1960. This was a six-lap standing-start race with eighteen riders divided into four classes, 125 cc, 150 cc, 175 cc and over 175 cc. The winner was J. B. Gamble on a 277 cc Maicoletta with an average speed of 54.29 mph (87.35 km/h). First in each class were: Don Noyes (175 cc class) on a 174 cc Heinkel, M. Brown (150 cc class) on a 145 cc Vespa GS and C. G. Peck (125 cc class) on a 124 cc Rumi. Before this time there had been numerous speed and endurance events but all clubs and organisations had carefully avoided the word 'race'. The events nearest to races before this were regularity trials, which

An endurance-racing Moto Rumi similar to the Bol d'Or winners. Rumi also manufactured production racing motorcycles using an identical motor, making it easy for the scooterists to tune their machines. Note the long-distance fuel tank and rocking pedal gear change.

The Lambretta Model B at Montlhery in 1950, when the 12-hour endurance records were established.

were long-distance events held on race-tracks in which riders had to lap consistently at a fixed average speed. Many of these regularity trials were run like races, as riders who had experienced mechanical problems tried to make up lost time.

During the 1950s and 1960s many feats were accomplished by scooters, both privately financed and with commercial sponsorship, the latter in order to boost sales of a particular make. Lambretta went to great lengths with factory machines, usually with the emphasis on speed. On 8th August 1951 Romulo Ferri took a series of world records at Montlhery, in the 125 cc class, on a supercharged, fully streamlined machine based on the C and LC models. The flying start kilometre record of 201 km/h (124.9 mph) survived for over twenty years and many 175 cc class records were broken on the same 123 cc machine. Even earlier

The Lambretta works record breaker based on the C model. This machine captured 53 world records in 1951.

TOP: *A 1956 Lambretta 150 D. Fully enclosed machines had become the norm by 1954 but this model was marketed first as an economy scooter and later as a sports machine. The motor had fan cooling borrowed from the enclosed LD model.*

CENTRE: *A Lambretta factory six-day trial machine of 1952. Note the aluminium endurance fuel tank, large cylinder finning and carburettor.*

BOTTOM: *A 1958 DKR Defiant with a 197 cc Villiers four-speed motor (9E). Despite the unusual style, with a fuel tank mounted in the front, the handling was excellent and top speed was 60 mph (97 km/h). The price in 1958 was £188 1s 3d.*

than this, Lambretta had taken the 12-hour duration record when a B model achieved 1592 km (989 miles) at an average speed of 132.6 km/h (82.4 mph). This machine was ridden by three riders, Ambrossini, Ferri and Rizzi, on 5th October 1950 at Montlhery.

One of the more bizarre achievements for Lambretta was Jeff Parker's ride, on a standard model D Lambretta, to the top of Ben Nevis. On 16th June 1957, Jeff Parker and Lewis More rode two new standard machines 340 miles (547 km) from Edinburgh to Fort William, in order to run them in before commencing the 4406 foot (1343 metre) climb. The two riders started the climb at 9 a.m., but at just over 2000 feet (610 metres), More had to retire with clutch slip. The temperature soared to over 80 F (26 C) but Jeff Parker reached the summit in five hours with a total climb, including wheel spin, of over 17 miles (27 km).

Innocenti strongly supported sporting activities and even entered works teams, consisting of three riders, in events such as the International Six Day Trial and the Welsh Three Day Trial. In 1961 Alan Kimber, a Lambretta works rider, won the scooter award in the Welsh Three Day Trial and completed the 1961 International Six Day Trial, covering 1200 miles (1931 km), while 86 motorcycles failed to finish the event.

Piaggio tended to be more conservative in their stunts, though in the early days Vespa sponsored world record-breaking attempts. Vespa looked more towards economy, reliability and flexibility, reflected in the following achievements. In 1952 Georges Monneret crossed the English Channel from Calais to Dover on a 125 cc Vespa mounted on floats and with a propeller driven by the rear wheel on a roller. Having landed at Dover, he disconnected the machine from the floats and rode it to a reception in London.

In 1955 one of the United Kingdom's foremost scooter dealers, Andre Baldet, made an unassisted climb of Snowdon on a 125 cc Vespa. He achieved this by carrying 100 pounds (45 kg) of sand on a front-shield carrier as ballast and made the climb without stopping the engine. In 1959 Joan Short and Tommy Behan of the Vespa Club of Britain rode a standard GS Vespa from London to Paris on £1's worth of petrol, whilst an American recorded over 30,000 miles (48,000 km) on a new Vespa, riding it across the United States, down to Mexico and back to New York, all within six months.

Other scooter manufacturers set out to prove that their models were capable of

Scooter sidecar racing offers all the thrills of motorcycle combination racing. Machines are now very specialised although motors still mostly originate from Lambretta.

Many scooterists enjoy modifying their machines either mechanically or cosmetically. This water-cooled and customised machine combines both forms of modification.

extraordinary performance. A German Maicoletta scooter, for example, covered 1062 miles (1709 km) around the TT course in 24 hours in appalling weather conditions.

Meanwhile DKR machines were used to prove that British scooters were as good as European ones. Andre Baldet and Dennis Christian used a DKR Manx 250 cc machine and in foul weather travelled 500 miles (804 km) in 500 minutes around the MIRA test track in March 1959. On 17th June 1960 two DKRs, one a Manx combination ridden by Flash Rogers with his eleven-year-old son, David, in the sidecar, the other a sole 200 cc Defiant ridden by Ken Bass, were ridden over 4000 miles (6437 km) from Castrol House, England,

Twenty-four-hour endurance racing became popular with scooterists. This Lambretta D racer carries a large fuel load in the specially fabricated aluminium tank, in order to reduce pit stops.

31

returning fourteen days later, having climbed all thirty-two major European passes, with three days rest in the middle.

These are only a few examples of the performance and reliability testing that went on in the 1950s and 1960s and which captured the imagination of scooter clubs, whose events became more and more ambitious. Large numbers of scooters entered the ACU National in Britain, which involved riding 600 miles (965 km) in 24 hours whilst checking into as many control points as possible.

Esso organised a 'Scoot to Scotland' annual event, which in 1964 had almost four hundred scooter competitors, whilst the Isle of Man Scooter Week consisted of five days of events, including a reliability trial around the TT circuit (the Manx 400), a sporting trial (similar to motorcycle endurance tests), a sprint along a twisty metalled road known as Druidale, a hill climb and sand racing. Manufacturers sponsored teams and dealers sponsored club entries to the extent that in 1968, for example, there were more than 550 riders.

Since the early 1950s Lambretta and Vespa in particular have promoted scooter club activity and this became an important part of scootering. Many of the events organised were competitive, creating rivalry between the clubs. Whilst scooter sales declined in the 1970s, the club activity has continued, particularly in Britain and Germany. In the following decades, although never repeating the volumes of the late 1950s and early 1960s, a sustained niche sport has continued without a break, while social scooter clubs, perhaps surprisingly, survived a dearth in available machinery after the Lambretta disappeared, leaving Vespa as the sole traditional scooter.

By the late 1950s scooter club outings would often involve a large number of riders descending on a tourist resort and parading through the town centre.

A THIRD GENERATION?

By the late 1960s Lambretta and Vespa between them virtually dominated the world scooter market, although this domination was to prove short-lived. Many potential customers in need of cheap transport, and influenced by the arrival of small affordable cars like the Mini, were lured into the comfort and better weather protection that a four-wheeled vehicle offered. As a result the demand for scooters declined significantly by the end of the decade. When sales of Lambretta and Vespa hit an all-time low in the 1970s, many people believed that the scooter would disappear altogether. Throughout western Europe a new affluence meant that most young people could afford to purchase a car as their first motor transport, thus removing one of the major reasons for buying a scooter.

Lambretta ceased production in Italy and for a few years Indian and Spanish models made under licence met the small demand from hardened Lambretta enthusiasts. Even the Vespa looked doomed when Piaggio seemingly believed its time was over and brought out a new scooter called the Cosa. Suddenly the two names that were practically synonymous with scooters were on the brink of extinction. The Indian and Spanish products never gained the ardent following of Innocenti Lambrettas and soon ceased production. However, Piaggio found that the Cosa was not going to be allowed to replace the Vespa. A strong lobby and a steady stream of customers remained loyal to the Vespa and as a result a rationalised and reduced Vespa range has sustained it in constant production for more than sixty years and appears to be retaining customer loyalty for further generations.

In the 1990s, after almost twenty years in the doldrums, scooters were about to regain

Innovation has always been a key factor in scooter design. BMW created the C1 in 125 cc and 176 cc (shown here) models as a two-wheel alternative to a car for commuting. BMW argued that a helmet was not needed, because the C1 had safety belts and protection hoops, but they were unsuccessful in changing British law. This contributed to poor sales and the model was produced only from 2001 to 2004.

Piaggio remains a major manufacturer of scooters of all sizes. Launched in 2004, the Gilera Nexus 500 cc offers performance that matches many mid-range modern motorcycles, attracting another group of customers to scootering. Cruising motorways at the maximum legal speed is relaxed and comfortable on such machines. This example is a 2006 model.

their popularity in a new and very different manner that would divide scooterists into two distinct factions, 'traditional' and 'twist and go'. The traditional market had stabilised to a steady but acceptable volume consisting of classic and traditional scooterists and their successors who fervently supported the scooter culture created over the previous forty years. These owners were more interested in fashion, scooter clubs and style than in practical economy.

The door was open for a new style of scooter that catered for alternative transport needs. Lightweight automatic scooters, initially in very small capacity (50 cc to 125 cc), began to find favour as a practical, economical and extremely easy to ride form of transport, suitable for crowded urban streets. Twisting the throttle open was all that was required to ride them, hence the description 'twist and go'.

The popularity of 'twist and go' scooters was given a major boost when a number of celebrities started using these ambitiously styled, simple to ride lightweights. The scooters of the 1950s and 1960s had received beneficial publicity when stars such as Ursula Andress, Marlon Brando and Cliff Richard began using them, thus promoting sales. So it was with the new automatics when a new generation of celebrities were seen to be riding them, including Leonardo Di Caprio, Jamie Oliver, Jay Kay from Jamiroquai, Sarah Jessica Parker, Jonathan Ross and Kevin Spacey. A common thread with the previous generation of scooterists was that image, rather than economy, was again a major factor, though it was a very different image to that of the traditional scooterist. Sales boomed again just as they had forty years earlier. Scooters were soon the height of fashion and in great demand from teenagers. Strong growth in sales generated a plethora of increasingly high-tech models, while the

Another innovative scooter design: with three wheels in this configuration, it was claimed that greater stability and better braking were offered, while the machine could stay upright without a stand. For cornering, the Piaggio MP3 (available as 125 cc and 250 cc machines) leans like a conventional scooter.

widespread use of plastic bodywork led to even more adventurous styling.

So now scootering had three distinct sectors. The first group was loyal to the traditional scooter (now reduced to only one brand of new machine, Vespa). The second group was the growing band of enthusiasts for vintage scooters, while the third was the 'twist and go' generation, who had never been part of the traditional or vintage scene and consisted mainly of fashion-following teenagers. For a short period, these three groups apparently had little in common but soon the capacity and performance of the automatics dramatically increased, led by machines such as the Gilera Runner (owned by Piaggio) in 180 cc two-stroke form. The Runner quickly achieved a respected status among all three groups as the traditional and vintage riders

discovered that it could surpass both the modern Vespa and vintage models in all measures of performance. With practical features such as under-seat storage (which could accommodate a full-face helmet) and a speed advantage of more than 10 mph (16 km/h) over the fastest Vespa, this scooter was to be at the forefront of the new 'upstart' generation of scooters.

With the last barriers to acceptability removed, 'twist and go' development was rapid. By the middle of the first decade of the twenty-first century, numerous manufacturers prospered and the automatic scooter grew in variety and size. The scooterist was once again spoilt for choice, with major manufacturers from Japan and other Asian countries, Italy, France and eastern Europe contributing to a vast and diverse range. Irrespective of whether

The 1999 Gilera Runner SP in 180 cc two-stroke form had a significant influence in making automatic scooters acceptable to traditional scooterists because of its exceptional performance (around 80 mph – 128 km/h – and superb handling). Environmental laws now make two strokes obsolete and this is the four-stroke VXR version produced from 2002.

a small economical urban commuter machine or a high-speed long-distance motorway cruiser was wanted, the third-generation scooter was available and affordable, delivering style, performance, excitement, practicality, ease of use, weather protection and comfort. Some even had a roof! Most importantly, the scooter now offered unrivalled congestion beating, a solution to inner city parking and street credibility.

Not content with winning over all types of scooterist, the makers of the third-generation scooters set their sights on a segment of the motorcycle market. Wheel sizes on motorcycles were being decreased at the same time as engine and wheel sizes on scooters were being increased, resulting again in the differences between the two becoming blurred. Manufacturers expanded their range to offer automatic scooters from 50 cc up to 650 cc which provided economy or performance close to those of any motorcycle of comparable

Using the same power plant as the Gilera Runner SP, this 180 cc Italjet Dragster was very fast and epitomised the flamboyant style and high-tech engineering customers expect from scooters in the twenty-first century.

36

The original 1946 style can still be recognised in this modern scooter. The 2007 250 cc Vespa GTS combines traditional looks with state of the art engineering to provide tradition, technology and performance in one machine.

size. Traditional motorcyclists were now being attracted to the ease of use and other advantages that the automatic scooter offered. Top speeds of over 100 mph (160 km/h) and distances of 600 miles (1000 km) per day have become realistic choices on larger machines while smaller ones retain their economy. Manoeuvrability, and cleanliness, ease of use and weather protection remain key factors that make the modern motor scooter a credible alternative to motorcycles of all sizes. Traffic congestion, lack of parking spaces and cost are again giving scooters an advantage over the small car. The difference in the twenty-first century is that people can generally afford cars but dislike the problems they are subject to. The scooter is often the choice to 'beat the traffic' and is frequently bought in addition to a car, not instead of it! In the past, just when their demise seemed inevitable, scooters have proved to be very adaptable and enjoyed a new lease of life. The latest generation may very well not be the last.

FURTHER READING

Brinson, Bev. *The Complete Idiot's Guide to Motor Scooters*. Alpha Books, 2007.

Brockway, Eric. *Vespa: An Illustrated Story*. Haynes Publishing, 1998.

Brown, Gareth. *Scooter Boys*. Virgin Books, 2006.

Dan, Mike. *A–Z of Popular Scooters*. Veloce Publishing, 2007.

Dregni, Eric, and Dregni, Brian. *The Scooter Bible*. Whitehorse Press, 2005.

Sarti, Giorgio. *Vespa: 1946–2006: 60 Years of the Vespa*. Motorbooks International, 2006.

Sparrow, David. *Motor Scooters: Colour Family Album*. Veloce Publishing, 1998.

Webster, Mike. *Classic Scooters*. Parragon Plus, 1997.

Woods, Bob. *The Scooter Book*. Hylas Publishing, 2004.

Whilst the two-stroke scooter is no longer manufactured for environmental reasons, this two-stroke Vespa has 'gone green' by being entirely covered with artificial grass.

SCOOTER CLUBS

Further information can be obtained from these national organisations.

British Scooter Sport Organisation (BSSO), 219 Elmers End Road, Beckenham, Kent BR3 4EH. Website: www.scooterracing.org.uk

Lambretta Club of Great Britain, 5 Dulas Close, Redcar, Cleveland TS10 2SJ. Website: www.lcgb.co.uk

Vespa Club of Britain, 19 Carriage Drive, Chelmsford CM1 6UY. Website: www.vespaclubofbritain.co.uk

Vintage Motor Scooter Club, 11 Ivanhoe Avenue, Lowton St Lukes, Warrington WA3 3HX. Website: www.vmsc.co.uk

Over fifty years old when photographed in 2007, this Goggo scooter is typical of the superb standards of preservation achieved by the large number of vintage scooter enthusiasts throughout the world.

PLACES TO VISIT

Scooters can be seen on display in numerous museums, large and small, throughout the world. Those listed below are a small sample but they include some that are dedicated to the scooter. Readers are advised to telephone before visiting to check that relevant items are on show, as well as to find out the opening times.

GREAT BRITAIN

Imperial War Museum, Lambeth Road, London SE1 6HZ. Telephone: 020 7416 5320. Website: www.iwm.org.uk

Lambretta Museum, 77 Alfred Street, Weston-super-Mare BS23 1PP. Telephone: 01934 417834. Website: www.lambrettamuseum.co.uk or www.scooterproducts.com

National Motor Museum, John Montagu Building, Beaulieu, Brockenhurst, Hampshire SO42 7ZN. Telephone: 01590 612345. Website: www.beaulieu.co.uk

National Motorcycle Museum, Coventry Road, Bickenhill, Solihull, West Midlands B92 0EJ. Telephone: 01675 443311. Website: www.nationalmotorcyclemuseum.co.uk

Sammy Miller Motorcycle Museum, Bashley Cross Road, New Milton, Hampshire BS25 5SZ. Telephone: 01425 616446. Website: www.sammymiller.co.uk

Science Museum, Exhibition Road, South Kensington, London SW7 2DD. Telephone: 0870 870 4868. Website: www.sciencemuseum.org.uk

EUROPE

Museo Scooter e Lambretta, Via Turati 7, Rodano, Milan, Italy.

Museo Piaggio (Vespa Museum), Viale Rinaldo Piaggio 7, 56025 Pontadera, Italy. Website: www.museopiaggio.it

The Portanje Scooter and Nostalgia Collection, 3981 AB41, Bunnik, Netherlands. Website: http://home.tiscali.nl/~cb003819 (Private collection. Visits on open days or by appointment only.)

RRRollipop, Hauptplatz 28, A3730 Eggenburg, Austria. Website: www.rrrollipop.at

Japanese manufacturers in the 1980s adopted space-age styling with widespread use of plastic bodywork. This 250 cc Honda is a typical scooter of the period.